Becoming The Best Big Sister Ever

by Lena Liz

Illustration by: Natalia Aksmit

This is my book.

My name is _____

Will you please read it to me?

Thank you.

Daddy announced: "The new baby is coming home today!"
I was so happy. I clapped, danced, and sang, "hip, hip, hooray!"

I am going to be the best big sister ever.

I will love and care for the baby forever.

But when the baby came home, I suddenly felt sad.

My sibling was stealing my mommy and my daddy!

But mommy gave me a hug and kissed my forehead.
"We will always love you the same." she said softly.

I felt a lot better and sat with the baby for a while.
All my worries vanished at the sight of baby's smile.

They sat in daddy's arms as snug as a bug in a rug.
The new baby laughed and gave my finger a big hug.

So I offered to help with all the baby tasks.
It was a lot for such a small baby to ask!

I love watching the baby laugh as I tickle their belly.

But I ran far, far away when things get too smelly.

When baby cries, screams, and wiggles all over the place.
I try to make them laugh by making my funniest face.

When baby yawns and starts rubbing its tired eyes.
I send them off to sleep with a sweet lullaby.

The baby loves it when mommy washes their hair.
But their splish-splashing gets water everywhere!

Feeding a baby is not always the easiest chore.

But going for walks in the park together. I adore!

I love picking out the baby's cutest clothes.

Sometimes I let the baby steal my nose.

I'm always there to make sure baby doesn't fall.
My sibling is my new best friend, after all.

I will be there to teach the new baby to walk.

And I will be there when the baby starts to talk.

I always fight away baby's fears.

And those who cause the baby's tears.

The baby and I will never be apart.

Because

I love

the new baby
with all my heart!

Dear reader

I hope you enjoyed reading this book. I will be grateful if you please spare a moment to drop a quick review on Amazon for us. In case of any concerns or suggestions you can freely ask at lenalizwrites@gmail.com or follow me on facebook and pinterest @lenalizwrites

About the Author

Lena Liz is an exciting author on her way up the career ladder while juggling a family and a blossoming career as a children's writer. It was the impending birth of her second child and coping with an anxious daughter who was concerned and confused about her role in the family with the coming of a new arrival that prompted Lena to seek a way to explain it. Her solution was to write a book and now she has one that she can proudly say has lived up to her expectations, as her own daughter became much more relaxed once she had read it a few times. Though, her ambitions are to write more books that help children understand the world around them.

About the Illustrator

Natalia Aksmit is a founder of an online Graphics Store, the art hub. Natalia and her team are passionate and creative when it comes to creating interesting art for children. For more than 15 years they have been providing eye catching illustrations based on a wide range of art. Natalia Aksmit lives in Ukraine with her family and she is passionate about providing quality art around the globe. For more details please follow on facebook @thearthub.

Made in the USA
Las Vegas, NV
23 November 2024

12500111R00019